Hallowed Manger Ground

A Christmas Musical for Every Choir

Arranged by Gary Rhodes and Cliff Duren

Contents

All Creation Sing (Joy to the World)	3
The Face of God	18
Silent Night! Holy Night!	29
Emmanuel (Hallowed Manger Ground)	33
King of All the Nations *with* Hark! The Herald Angels Sing	44

PUBLISHING COMPANY

LILLENAS.COM

All Creation Sing
(Joy to the World)

Words and Music by
STEVE FEE
Arr. by Gary Rhodes

*MALE NARRATOR: Welcome to Bethlehem . . . a town with a
rich history. It was of this small town the prophet Micah said,
"But you, O Bethlehem, are only a small village among all the
people of Judah. Yet a ruler of Israel will come from you, one
whose origins are from the distant past." (Micah 5:2 NLT para)*

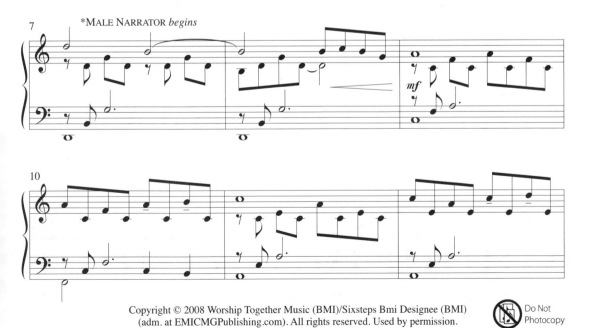

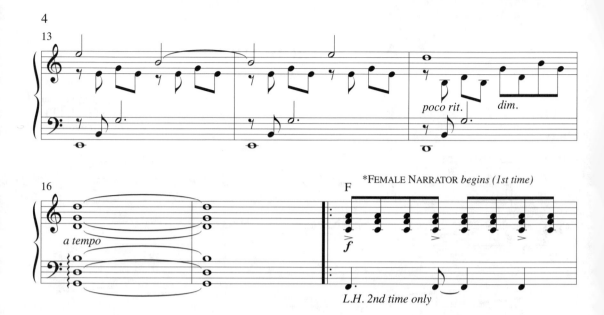

*FEMALE NARRATOR: Now the prophecy has been fulfilled. A humble carpenter named Joseph and his wife Mary have traveled here to register for the census, and Mary has given birth to her firstborn son.

**MALE NARRATOR: Oh yes, the story is familiar and yet always new. It's the story of the inn that had no room, and the angel that brought good news to the shepherds. It's the sky filling with angels praising God, and those shepherds stumbling down the Bethlehem hillsides and into that sleepy town.

***FEMALE NARRATOR: It's a baby, wrapped in swaddling clothes . . . Heaven's gift to the world . . . God with us . . . Emmanuel. And most of all, it's a story of joy.

MALE NARRATOR *begins (1st time)* ***FEMALE NARRATOR** begins*

(to pg. 4, meas. 18)

CD: 2

CD: 29

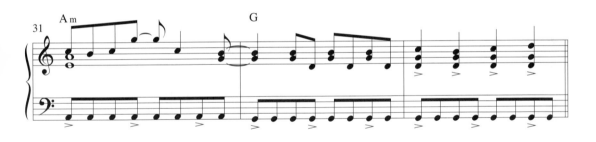

CHOIR *unis.*

Joy   to   the world!   the— Lord— is—

6

CD: 4
CD: 31

59

the won - ders!
the won - ders of His love!

the won - ders!

61

He rules the world with truth and
With truth and

He rules the world with truth and

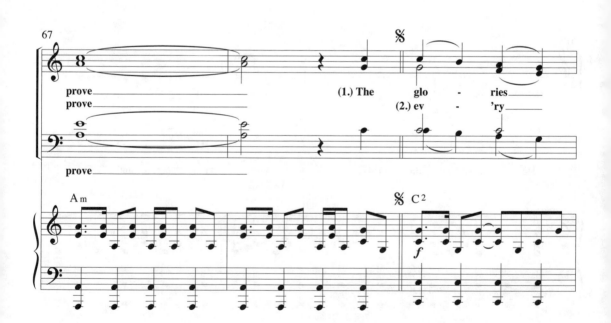

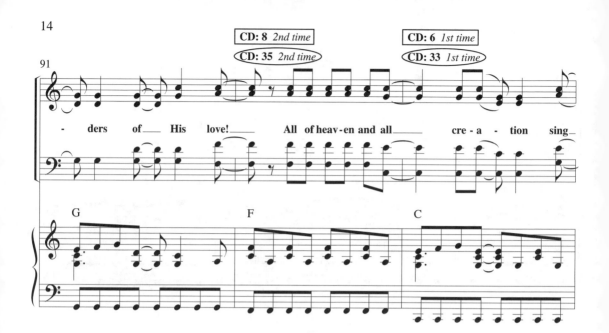

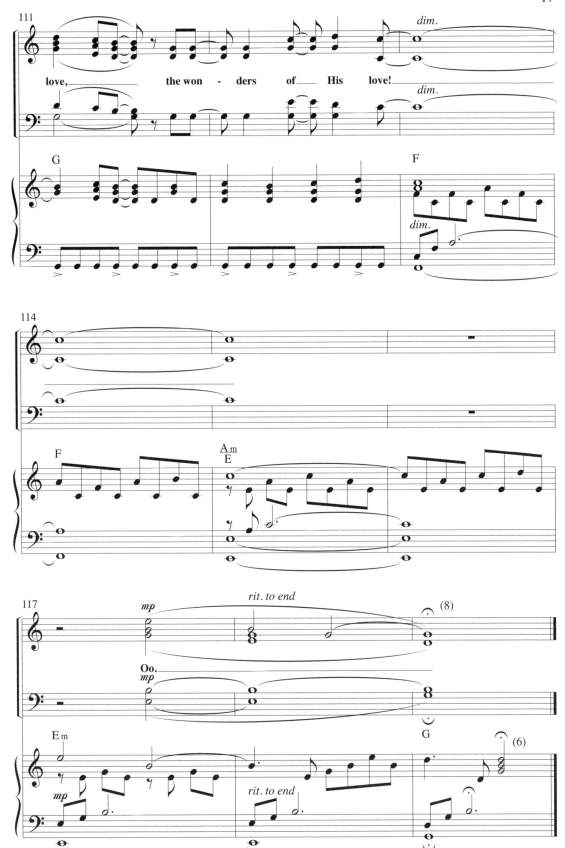

The Face of God

Words and Music by
PHIL MEHRENS and DAVE CLARK
Arr. by Cliff Duren

FEMALE NARRATOR: *(Without music)* Just like every new mother,
Mary must have gazed in wonder at her tiny son—a precious baby
like so many others, and yet unlike any child ever born. *(Music begins)*
She knew He was a miracle, but could she have imagined that when
she held Him close, she was looking into the very face of her Creator?

PLEASE NOTE: Copying of this product is NOT covered by CCLI licenses. For CCLI information call 1-800-234-2446.

earth and the sky.___ These are the ears___ that

CD: 10
CD: 37

lis - tened as an - gels gave us the prom - ise I'm

hold - ing to - night._____

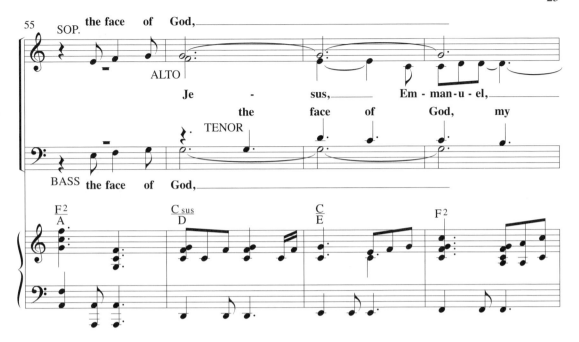

MALE NARRATOR: *(Without music)* The night Jesus was
born changed everything. He came into a world of darkness
and brought light.

(Music begins)

FEMALE NARRATOR: Into the chaos, He brought peace.
Into the silence, He brought rejoicing.

MALE NARRATOR: And into the searching, He brought hope.

Silent Night! Holy Night!

JOSEPH MOHR

FRANZ GRUBER
Arr. by Gary Rhodes

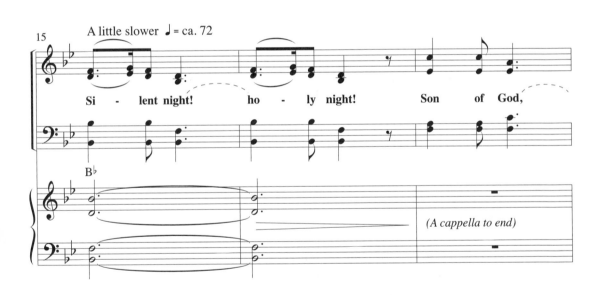

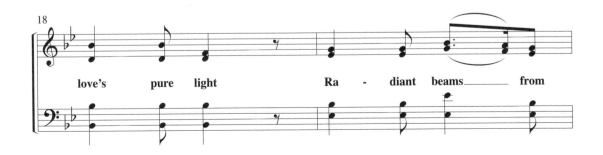

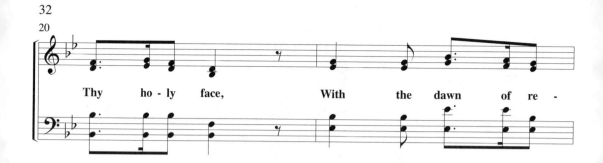

Thy ho - ly face, With the dawn of re -

deem - ing grace, Je - sus, Lord, at Thy

birth,_____ Je - sus, Lord, at Thy birth.

MALE NARRATOR: *(Without music)* The manger was the most
humble of beds for Heaven's King. But God would not allow
the birth of His Son to go unnoticed. There would be a new
star in the sky to honor His arrival. *(Music begins)* There
would be wealthy scholars who would journey long to find
Him, and they would bring their gifts and their worship.

Emmanuel
(Hallowed Manger Ground)

Words and Music by
CHRIS TOMLIN and ED CASH
Arr. by Gary Rhodes

Praise His name, Em - man - u -
el!
The Son of God,__ here, born to__ bleed;__ A crown of thorns__ would

CD: 20
CD: 47

84

el._____ God in - car - nate, here to_____

el._____

D♭ A♭/C A♭/D♭ D♭6 A♭/E♭ B♭m/E♭

88

dwell!_____ Em - man - u - el, Em -

Em-man - u - el, O praise__ Em -

E♭ A♭ E♭

91

man - u - el._____ Praise His

man - u - el._____

A♭/C D♭ A♭/C

FEMALE NARRATOR: *(Without music)* Emmanuel. God is with us. What a miracle of love and grace. Because God came on that first Christmas, we have a Savior. We can be forgiven, and everything that destroyed our fellowship with God can be erased.

MALE NARRATOR: Because God is with us, death is conquered and fear can't win. The sorrow we experience in this life is temporary, and our pain is only for a moment.

(Music begins)

FEMALE NARRATOR: Because God is with us, joy is possible.

MALE NARRATOR: Peace is attainable.

FEMALE NARRATOR: And glory is inevitable.

MALE NARRATOR: So sing out today! Give Him the honor He deserves. Join with the angels in proclaiming His birth.

King of All the Nations

with

Hark! the Herald Angels Sing

CHARLES WESLEY
and AMANDA SINGER

FELIX MENDELSSOHN
and AMANDA SINGER
Arr. by Amanda Singer,
Ray Jones and Brian Duncan

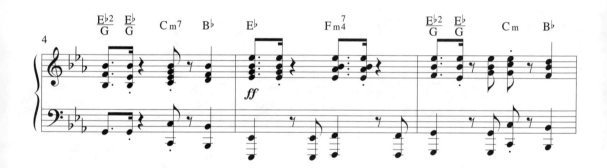

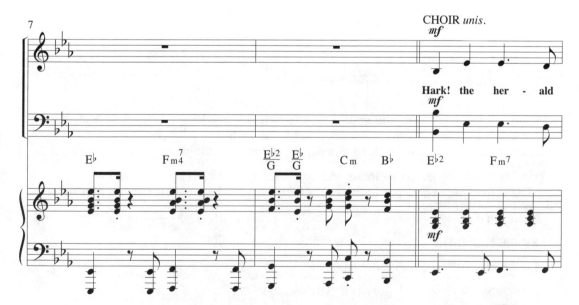

CD: 24
CD: 51

37

Late in time be-hold Him come—— Off-spring of the

E F#m7 E2/G# F#/A# G#m7 F#/A# B

40

vir-gin's womb. Veiled in flesh the God-head see;——

E M7 F# B E2 C#m7 F#m7 C#m/F# C#m/B B/A

43

Hail th'in-car-nate De-i-ty,—— Pleased as man with

G#m7 C#m F#m7 C#m/B B A C#7b9

King of all___ the na - tions, we bring___ You___ praise!_____ King of our___ sal - va - tion; Je - sus,___ You___ reign!

CD: 26
CD: 53